THRONE
FALCON
EYE

THRONE
FALCON
EYE

Poems by
Hugh Seidman

Vintage Books
A Division of Random House
New York

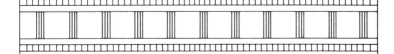

FIRST VINTAGE EDITION, SEPTEMBER 1982

The poems in this book were originally published, some in different form, in the magazines listed below.

"However Often" originally appeared in *The American Poetry Review*. "Zero" and "Ode to the Republic" originally appeared in *Ironwood*. "The Ill" and "Eurydice" originally appeared in *Poetry*. Other selections appeared in the following publications: *Beloit Poetry Journal, Granite, Gravida, Living Hand, Madison Review, Occurrence, The Ohio Review, Paris/Atlantic, The Paris Review, Pequod, Some Other Magazine, Sun, Unmuzzled Ox,* and *The William and Mary Review*.

Hardcover edition published simultaneously by Random House, Inc.

Library of Congress Cataloging in Publication Data
Seidman, Hugh, 1940–
Throne/falcon/eye.
I. Title.
PS3569.E53T4   1982b   811'.54   82-40041
ISBN 0-394-71045-2   AACR2

For my Mother and Father

Luego, haciendo del átomo una espiga,
encenderé mis hoces al pie de ella
y la espiga será por fin espiga.

—*César Vallejo* (*"Marcha Nupcial"*)

CONTENTS

1

EMBARKMENT

Is this yet to be the freight of Claude Lorraine

The gold of Sheba for a king's ennui
before his thousand wives and concubines
across the archaic night sea

Is this yet to be the anachronous Greek cartoon
calipered to the columns' groove

Are these sunbursts yet to be the blind
scalpels that would sign
below the breasts of the fleshed sky
to fit the heart into the body to survive

O surely I do not like to care or to not care
that the passage of the soul
takes on some second-rate nubile queen

Although I do not seem to turn the blade
from the prose of these rapes and revulsions

Perhaps it is how steel must remember the vein
or how sleep must unwind the bandages of the Pharaohs
who refuse to die
unclaimed as the shadows on their stones

But is this yet to be the reply
to the body drugged under the dawn as if alive
as the clouds ride slowly through the rooms

Is this yet to be the verdict under the ductile beams

That a slave must be chained into the ribs
to beat like the heart of the figurehead
whose nipples spread the waves of that sea

That a rower must sweat under the sun's day in the hold
so that she can sail in the dream
on the dream of that sea

EURYDICE

But still after seven years I met you again like a movie
by accident in the street:
a psychologist, a mother
still tall with small feet
still to be called beautiful
dark haired yet with one gray streak
as if the human had marred the human

But still it was hard not to smile
that lovers died or that death went on
like a life or that we
lived again before the blue steel
toy angel of your new daughter
who was yours and no man's
though I slept like a husband and wore your bone ring

And still the gulls glinted
and we fed the ducks and horse
on Amagansett's white beach
and still any wind blew the clouds
at the abandoned elevated road in the dusk on the Hudson
where the bulbs were screwed
as to the metal of some war

And still you asked what I thought
whatever I thought I thought
and your daughter played doctor
when nothing seemed wrong but that
you stood at the yellow chrysanthemum
I held on her birthday
like all that you must not take

Or as when a woman takes anyone
to return to men as you said
that I had you to have nothing
whatever you said I withheld
to dream myself barred with the dead
at my barred crib
on Spring Street and on Water Street and on Ocean Avenue

So that the abstract dark grew
particular as of no particulars
like the shadows on the floor
or like that man and that woman
who still woke to the dawn
from whatever had been mammal
to thirst with the first salt of the reptile

Whatever love raged as to cure
love's second failure from the personal
blasphemy of its metaphors:
like the sun as the great
black arachnid in the tree
to track men by their vibrations
or like the dark on the stone in its blast that had been a man

Though you wrote in my book: *for H against despair*
and the mystical blue of your eye
like a chip of the air
still sparked in the room
whether of the mind or actual
close, total, yet unfathomable
as the glitter that was the sea

Or as the terror and the awe
of your body as your body
of whatever sent us back to the underworld

whatever hope meant or to yield
that you hung up in the dark when I called
whatever the dark was that blew
up an image to the enormous shining
like some dead actress in some dark theater on the screen

THE POOL

It is the stone not
its aura that lights me
to drop where you must
being of it

I admit I want to sink
I want that blindered
sleep under the brass
factored on your depth

As the oldest martial
of the fathers of
the tadpoles fat as mice
who bang the tiny drums

Where your arms take
the shadows to shadow
that would snatch me
though you easily swim

So then the pines
march against the sky
and before the windy
armies of the ripple

And the little waves
that grind and grind
the moon to your skull
startled at the rock

Nixie—
washing your breasts
in the starlight
and your small veined wings

MUSE

Men are hammering themselves into the steels of the spirit

Darling, or do you want the obelisk
the coherent urn, of course

The lead rhetorics are my mottoes too or should I say
that we sculptors know a lady or that

I love to pass time where the monoliths rot

But it continues does it not
beyond pro or con where what we might have been inflames
the bronze to take you as it goes

Ah, good-by!

Now you are like the ideal of a shadow
like the blank metals of the dark that long to be struck
into the coins of light

THE IMMORTAL

The ferry heaves past the buoys
the island spruce stand
straight to the universe

The dawn sea burns with phosphorus
I think the Milky Way's
immense dust

On a deck like this one
one hero had been chained
to steer the song

Many too have tried to clear
to be returned like his men
upon the body

For at that sky I can hear
your pitch beyond the current
so tuned to the lured

Or you were the Amazon
your nipples like flints
that spark under the hands

You were the gold-eyed
soldier of the mammal
who wails for the hull of rib

Or then you grew archaic
like the arachnid
or the stark blind fish

Or you were nothing but the air
the blue metal shield
and what you knew I knew

Of the whole wind
as if you would always be
love past the human

Like the mud
and the mineraled knife
in your hair for the initiate

Where the light strikes rock
at the coast like a fact
of what belief assures

Though you are only a woman
come down to the dock
common as a goddess

As I stand like all heroes
where the precise bee
whines at the screen

Because in the world
all men have seen
she who rules the world

Strict as rock
like you who are always empty
like you who are always full

And the sun flecks the tide
and the cormorants glide
on the drafts of the air

And the trees are at peace
the trees are at peace
or so it is said

And so

HOWEVER OFTEN

However often the stream was assessed
the leaves noted
the flowers, fishes, mammals of whatever country

However often the bee raged
or the dragonfly soared

However often the haze burned off
or bled through the miles of dawn

However often the pig squealed under the whole summer
or the mushroom spored

However often the spider built and rebuilt

However often the road was eroded
or the hill shimmered
medieval blue

It should have been possible to recall
all the aeons
all the ooze and bones

It should have been possible to reconstruct
the total arcanum
from only one of your cries

ZERO

The unbroken lake creaks
but a rat snaps in the trap
and thumb skin cracks and bleeds

And once I jabbed a fish-hole
and the black birds
bud oddly on the trees in the furnace cold

And the cloud rim is fire
and the ice in space freezes harder
and the astral TV flickers

But already a kitten can break a back
but now the cat is in the sack
and now I torch her corpse

And now I taste the air
for the sacrificial eye, ear, nose, anus
and the untranslatable genital

Until I make the monotonous still light
glitter like a fur
I stroked and stroked

To dull the edge of moon
as if the quick cut sealed slowly
to just teach a lesson

But still a cat glows
but now I breathe like the molecular
like the scar of the gill

And now I touch myself
like all dumb things at the ice-hole
who do not know why they know

THE WASP AND THE SPIDER

We came to his rage
though he was often
his own defeat

Out of the lust
for the brute country
or the impenetrable sky

We were naked when
the beavers slapped
their tails at the falls

And our shadows
glided the shallows
at the intense green

The gorge was his shore
though we touched
that empire

And the tree split
by the lightning to rot
and the leaves one by one

And the sun splayed
from the dawn at rock
where the fungi thrived

Though he hovered
as if magnetized
at her web like a radar

Where she weaved
as she would soon at me
unhealed and alive

Arachnid of your molt
reborn of divorce
as if you had never been

From the blast at the bed
from the festered gas
from the magnesium

Like the hand that hated
the arm in my dream
but what was that

But my mother's
black coin purse dangled
once on its string

To the yard at the drone
as still I tensed
and his wing

Shone under the cobalt
at her actinal pole
like an X ray of bones

Little monk who erected
the kingless throne
little needle of her north

Little nest seed
whose force was flight
at the fate of nest

Little tongue, little
acetylene at her belly
some still called love

Between the husks
of his brothers
and the novas of their cells

While the beavers
built and fueled
at the isotope of mud

As if we had dived
like our shadows
to the underwater rooms

As if we had been instinct
that silk and sting
yet whom but ourselves

ANGEL

On the E train a gargantua as fat as two men
as though no odder than whatever man to men
scratched his crotch and picked his nose

Beside a girl like a barbarian in polar bear
off up the escalator past the faces and fluorescents
as on a film prop to heaven

Such tar-pit tiger, such ancestral shark
such absolute zero of platinum below white
such reflection like ocean in the plate glass

So that I thought how men had crawled like men
to be burned on the land under the glare
as from a passion unknown in heaven

For now the street surged but what was lust to life
as frail as her parents had seen her
but how should I have stopped

How should I have been my own parent
how should I have said *death* to death
or put the mouse under the foot of the mammoth

CULT OF ISIS

1 Osiris

I had been taught his scattered life
cut upon her stele and her gate

I had learned that grotesque song
where the crab flamed over his phallus on that ground

I had felt him atone
to that heroine of the mummy
and how he had hinged to her like the gate

So drained I had veered
toward the ritual breasts like animals

I had taken the order to navigate
the shroud I could not leave
until we beached the final shore

I had borne him before the masked absolute mother
weeping upon the mouth of Egypt

And yet still she sneered fate
still I was made to make
the grave face of the son

And to kneel to this Lord-To-Be-Torn
upon the desert's annual body of her blood

2 Solitaire

The royal couples dream in their sarcophagi
though this is never their Egypt

Nor does she awake them
nor do they face each other

Beyond the door
the crotch of the aspen that weds the moon
trembles in its windy flesh

The stars are the grave candles
where the wildflower
impales the night

Though there is nothing of it in the play
before the dark women

Where winning is never to win
or the black Jack-Of-Errantry lies buried
under the two-faced
Queen-Of-Hearts

3 *Concubine*

How much is enough to pay or too much
or not enough, sphinx:
fur in the alley at Thebes, forget
the ascetic Aton sun

The eye is etched black at the brow
of gold below the jeweled scorpion
or the aquiline nostril
is offered in profile

As under the gallery's fluorescents
an edge of face talc
glints like a scar, sleek
art-deco cat guardian
exacting the curse of the tombs

She is enterable always
to the oldest paint of semen and blood
of the oiled immaculate
under the tindery silk

She, who has set the snake on Pharaoh's head
and bloomed the sand's
revenge and dismemberment
from the ennui of mud

But behind the tint eyelids
the drugged Great Mother steams in the plans
for quick profit
that instructs her to work, that
she is an artist

You may note the oddly voluptuous
carved nipple not unlike
the casually beringed
in green on the couch drinking daiquiris
while her thigh is stroked

It is everywhere the agony
of the masculinized jade goddess led
by the priests to her people
on their feast days of greed

Where on the lands from her morgue pavilions
her children feed past odyssey
of their thingness
before the lust and the rage
at that insensible stone

4 Bar

Let the light be the gilt sistrum
let any waitress be Egypt's sixty centuries

Let Thoth-Ibis judge the isolate mercifully

Let the singer sing love's cliché decade
like youth and death in that country

But if there is another song of the breast
as the breast and the body
that is bought for its art
or for art as the body only and not the nipple
lipsticked or the smeared rouge

If in another quest
the novice knows Pharaoh's house as lost to the desert
that he only shall cross

Is he thus not now crossing it
and is not its virgin now almost only thought

Like the statue to her myth where the drinker sits
where no song helps him and no breast

5 *Element*

It is 3500 B.C.
certain glyphs are so old they are now indecipherable
yet revered and inscribed

The high hawk
Falcon-Lord of all the Nile and Heliopolis
bears the solar disc and the snake
above the years

In fifty-four centuries Whitman will sing him as the self
dazzling and tremendous

At 5 A.M. the light is a blue shrill cry
over the sleeper
mourning upon the science to be called
She-Who-Martyrs-Egypt

It is 8000 B.C.
a hawk with a blood-eye grips a snake in its claw
though I am so borne by the weight of it
I cannot stand

Anywhere
the others breathe the secret
knowing no secret but
that to believe her as the secret is the exile

But how may we not believe

As Ra's eye had wandered from the ocean
as the dreamer had awakened
as had Whitman or the scribe who had worked the day
reborn or not under the sun

LOVE POEM

When one had left me I met you
but one you had left punched my eye
as his had been by one and so on

They stitched me in St. Vincent's
where a child yelled blood-eyed
though my jaw shut to a world

Where husbands shot husbands
and men in dark glasses had no eyes
and women broke men's glasses

Accidently but *bitch* they cried
though even Odin plucks an eye
to drink the well for a thirst

For always we swear rebirth
and the sticks change the *I
Ching*'s K'UN the earth-cunt to PEACE

As I should have sworn to you
that who could fail me but I
even if you picked me to goad him

Whose punch you assumed from men
that made my black, red eye
and my face for days like the meat

Like the ugly, stupid, blind
that takes an eye for an eye
though you had made me beautiful

Just as that world that blurred in
my left eye cleared in my right eye
yet it was the one world

CHAKHCHARAN, AFGHANISTAN

The fallen child drops its hollow cheek on its hand
it parts its caked lips
it sips from the puddle

It begs for the mutton fat
it picks the rice from the dirt
and nibbles the toxic root that bloats shut its face

Lambs slaughtered
sixteen million fur coats lost for export
seed wheat eaten, plowing bullocks butchered

A son sold for grain
when there is not grain
not a doctor for the sick who cannot eat the drugs

Some wheat seeps from America
but the trucks are scarce, the mountains blocked
the officials bribed, the army reluctant

So here life chooses
the dead now dead at last without irony:
objects, things past tears or food

Guilty as the fetus
who mimics and mimics them
as if to learn the inescapable body

COUPLETS

I said I would not write
Like W.C. Fields, juggler, dropping tennis balls in whites.

I would not make the peasant's cut
be more than cane to buy the yachts.

I would not make their suffering mine.
I was no rhyming bourgeoisie.

But in the movie where we kissed
my cheap Winchester glowed and left no taste.

Though Fields peeled a Habana—
too strong for me to smoke a fire?

The moral was too banal that we quarreled
like the mainland and the island.

Though Fidel upraised you when you fell,
cutting sugar, on your skull.

But now some Weatherman comes in out of the rain.
And some *gusano* sells cocaine.

And I puff a Monte Cristo at Elaine's
where the FBI now never takes a name.

And Fields is still a tippler, red-nosed at a bar,
and blue as any TV news or war.

So that I think that we were that:
just soldiers of the army, lean or fat.

And below the stars I miss you in my bed
till the sun comes like a warhead.

Like love that flares to solitude
beyond the evil and the good.

And yet shall form Fidel and Fields
as useless as cigars we furl to burn.

As thus I scribble with a will
how some blaze while others smoke to kill.

THE BATS

Something archaic that strafes
The white pine in the dusk at seven at the settling light

And the arched sweet cat rubs my legs
Claws and jumps at the chair

Pivots to fix the chipmunk at the oak near the beheaded robin
So between the dark and the dark

Like the unfurled membranes of the unborn
Let the world be the world

I mean guilt and the moral
For I too hunger when I eat the meat

Where the mouse broods in its nausea
When the cat breathes over the mousehole

And the worm excretes its moral of the wars—
But from the galactic whorls

From the nebulae of the fingerprints of his compassion
God will not stop us

Where the moth shines in his pupa
Where the ant marches his arduous floor

Where the maggot eggs are his axioms of the root
That the apple seeds or rots

AGENT ORANGE

At 400 rads the liver perforates
on two-hour doses of Thorazine and liquid morphine the
    Great Sphinx
seeps from the fat into the blood

And a man flies to the moon to leap like a boy with a robot's
    fervor
beyond the trumpets for war
in the oxygen heavy as decimals

I do not assume victim or victor
but often the light has a dark
like the inhaled sun over the gunships that stained the jungle

So that in ten years the night of the high school prom begins
    to glow
like a vast angel in a coma
though there are no angels

Though the spike-heeled Asian
girls go blind counting them on the microchips for the missiles
    buried
on the prairies like hieroglyphs

And the Pentagon and Dow Chemical
claim to have shown the lost wings of Rin-Tin-Tin and
    George Washington
to a corpse's wife and dog

And in the dark his children huddle over the luminous
    video games
to repulse the galactic hordes
like the first living archangels

THE BUS

Deaf twins in blue skirts who sign and grunt
but I love that the wrinkled white socks of one
sag to sneakers while her sister's stretch
from black patent leather toward skinny thighs

But two men snicker as if they were safe
from the red-shag beard on the madman I saw
wrapped up last summer like a sack on the pier
or who chopped the air like a headsman

And the retarded girl gives her token
though the driver knows she has lost her pass
and the fingerless white-haired black man
must pay but hides his stump at the coin box

But how shall I judge whoever maims a man
when I too thank God for my ears and hands
and to be as sane as the tearless sun
though how is it all have drunk of a mother

ODE TO THE REPUBLIC

Lit post card deco Empire
State, World Trade, City Corp,
Gulf + Western
monolith, glyph, magnet that aligns the dark.

Fame says: so many but so few
harsher than pneumatic drills. Gull
turds, soap
opera. Fair, says the weather. Coppery

Hair, luster of the pancake and blusher, blue
eyes, blue moon, draped fur on the bar
stool, rings
on the answering machine. But what can a dog

Do? Piss and scratch, bark and sleep
sixteen floors over the park. 6:02
on the SONY digital
flash. Gladiatorial stone lions,

Zoo monkey, cat, squirrel, sparrow,
pigeon, roach, rat, dumb horse
yoked to the oats
at the Plaza. Silver bars, gold ingots.

Knowledge is power the motto said on my parents'
wall. All this ark, exile, Circus,
home. Imagine
the great Roman eagle over the world.

A capitol on a planet
in a galaxy, in a universe, and you its citizen, citizen.

THE LANGUAGE

It was given to me
I did not choose it

Under the holy Bo-tree
the naked Buddha does not talk

All of the words of the world
do not change this

Now I tell you
now I speak

ARS POETICA

for the poet **RD**

The blind boy taped you and we clapped
starving beak after crumbs
hoarse with cancer and one breast
wrapped like a broken arm
where the oxygen tank
stood like a green soldier

You had liked my work, fed me cake
thin, hawk-nosed Italian:
aristocratic, unpublished
astrologer of four thousand poems
persisting as a typist
or on tiny grants

But how could an editor have seen
your unsent books
or had they grown like bonds
when the poor poets read
on your fold-up chairs
as if failure were wealth

As once you ignored me for months
so that I thought of my mother
who had replayed days like war
for me and my father
or who had answered our door
with a commando's paranoia

But how could I have explained
your lung on the X ray
clouded with the breath

that you had held so long
or that I never went back
to see you after I clapped

Though I mourned with a rigor
like your daughter and sons
as if for myself
at your body burned to bone
because you had nothing
when you might have had what?

Though how could I have lifted
the sky from your chest
or asked your forgiveness
from what untouched rage
at your name now black on the bell
where each day had flared

For inside was the dark
like a moral that the muse
was never to be spared
the pride of her children
though I heard your choice:
I had no courage not to write

And still the blind boy's dog moaned
and you wept to your flesh
thinner than beaten gold
that a breath might have torn
and still I shut my blinds
as you had at your work

And your death taught its debt
who escaped your life?
for you did not absolve me

and I wrote as my fourth grade student had
of his anorexic sister:
Fire is like a dead person

And your ashes blew to breath
for what was death but words
to break the tree and rock
but still the leaves fell
like what alphabet
to make you my muse in that dark

THE MOTHER

Ultimate, white-haired
bandaged at the eyes like Judgment
you lie at the hospital stainless faucets and the pipes
under a TV bolted to the ceiling

Though in 1946 at my aunt's when I was six
and as when I had been born
you came back from the mental ward in brown curls
and white anklets and blue pinafore
to the lavender hydrangeas

But yesterday on West Street like a supplicant
I crossed the cobbles where the rain
struck a woman under the girders
who raised her white shirt
for the truckers on the docks

So that again I sensed that son
whom his cousins had taunted to sullenness
for whatever the psychiatrists said
of you who could not care for him
ugly or beautiful as the prostitute

Though of course
I was ludicrous to compare her to you—
you who had warned me never to open the door to strangers
who had raved that men would kill you

You to whom I offer the water and the Chap Stick
for lips dry as a grandmother's
that curse your nurse and cataract

but bless my father past anger
forty years from the electroshock

And then you press your palms to your breasts
and tell me to forget
though you do not say what—

And then you are yourself, abstract
blank as the prehistoric groove in the cave
as if men had had a purpose like my hands
though I could not appease nor smooth nor heal you

THE FRONT

Out there, out there
he is not yet come
home from the moony peep show
or from the broiled meat
cut lean as the dead bones
so that a son may eat

Where a mother counts and cleans
the meat bones
again, again
for the soup for an only son
because a son
must be healthy
wealthier than a Jew-skeleton

Though she feeds him
no sweet:
that which would be worse
than to be dead
he is good and must eat the good
raw milk, vitamins
and his wheat bread, every day
and the broiled meat

She knows he will eat
or it is quick, quick to bed
to make no noise that might wake
a father and mother
while they lie dead

He has his eyedrops
and the compress for his head
and his wool scarf
and the enema
for naughty hands taught
where they are not to be

And how old is he
as old as the dead?
or the fur chubby teddy
he cuddles to sleep
or the yellow-soft rabbit who creeps
O bunny
will they broil *you*?

But listen, O listen
he beamed only to be their sun
their bright *one*
younger than one, two, or anything
new but mother's hero
in the old bad world

As you might have
to have had a father coo
don't cry, don't cry
we hear you through the stone
our sonny who plays alone
so sad he can't come home

Out there, out there
near pigeon at the tree
until the war is done
past time to tell the news

THE BEST THING

To speak each word
this is the best thing
to know another for no reason
this is the best thing

Another thing is the absent
plate, fork, spoon
with the sun going down
for its reasons

Though it is all to be read:
night, day, silence, breath
each so reasonable
that is so unreasonable

All but grief
the unexpected guest
always the last to sit
always the one for whom the place is to be set

SONG

Money talks
nobody walks

When I was young
my father bought
a *Rose Royce*
or so I thought

And at his left
I seemed to drive
though fathers knew
fathers thrive

As now I own
a handsome car
and father is
where fathers are

From sun to sun
though roses change
to prove sons ride
like sons again

For none will find it
odd I know
that my son drives me
to and fro

As if the roads
were hammered gold

to take a son
as roses go

To fall or lean
from pure green

THE ILL

for Jane

My father at eighty daily escapes my senile mother
and their four-room world she will not escape
where the Verrazano vaults the world

And on Canal Street his fat boss of the Real Estate Masons
sneers to him on a cigar where the wall peels:
"From poems your son lives?"

He had me at forty and I wagged like his "mutt"
though Aunt Ann found her "psychotic" on Ocean Parkway
while I lay home alone in my crib

And at our lunch he nods: "In the world men work"
(yet proud I do no "shit-work"?) as he had
but with no regret: "If only Mother had been well"

But now he collects rents where the Puerto Ricans sweat
whose own Polish mother had stitched
when he was six for second class to New York in Nineteen-Six

And my mother's Polish father had ground lenses in Carolina
and when I was a "bad boy" she would scold:
"*I* nursed my mother while Aunt Ann danced"

But now she nags and nags: "Are you happy or in love?"
because she bore me like the funnel of the ocean
though if my father dies I will commit her

"As if," I say madly, "she lives too long"
for she forgets all that I tell her
though once she was the "crackerjack" steno for Uncle George

Though some say there were fathers who make mothers "mad"
and sons who ask too much
so that the rage of love was not love but a madness

Though both will leave me as I was found
that day my father left work to "mother" me
who I dream slams my eggs on the table late for his work

Though I do not cry that she is gone
as if it is my fault this is his meal
God knows, my poor mother, for the wages of what work in
    the world

GRAVE

When you want to unstop
my tub or phone
the plumber as if
I cannot or we compete

For a waitress's
laugh I think amazed
how Odin stoops
in your little gray

Hat who soaped me
when mother was depressed
yet your priestess
whom now no drug

Keeps from the Utica
Masonic Old Age Home
even as the dark
would never set on

Your own mother's
stone as it bends you
even as you had knelt
to raise your own

Father on his bed
or told me: *be strong*
I Thor who hammered
your nails or drove

Your car though I groan
to help you up
heavy as bones
for already I squat

So small in the bath
and you are so marked
like the one-eyed
Odin by the dark

Your back to the light
like a negative
of a light against
the dark in the mind

As pale as Yggdrasil
at the cock-crow
in heaven and hell
though who could have

Washed a son more
tenderly who loved
the maimed gods you taught
though I was ever

The stubborn, dull boy who
could not learn: *father
you are my body
foretold as stone* ·

KADDISH

O TORAH TORAH TORAH
downtown but uptown
and in gold on black bronze and lead:
This Obelisk Shall Outlast

O Dream Dream Dream
yet I fasted not nor atoned
I made no tabernacle
on Tish'a Be'ab with Solomon

O Mitzvah Mitzvah Mitzvah
I faked the Hebrew
I the circumcised
stubborn as the metal

O Life Life Life
I yelled to the *mohel*'s knife
I bewailed myself
like any for the dead

O Jew Jew Jew
of God's pagan blood
I was a man in a blue suit
suede shoes and gold ring

O Israel Israel Israel
though I had no tribe
and my parents lay
under the bronze and lead

O TORAH TORAH TORAH
uptown but downtown
but O father, O mother
who would mourn Zion if you were dead

ON TV

After forty years Poland's sky is still sky
over the tourist museum
of her barrack at Birkenau

But in 1945 she saw twenty thousand a day
gassed from the cattle cars
the ovens blazed night and day

So that I remember King David's gold star
stuck to my coat and my arm tattooed
though I live unmarked

I mean: I would be dead
had not my grandparents fled in 1906
and I am no Jew but for my body from God

But she was made nude before the SS
so orthodox she fasted on Tish'a Be'ab
and refused bread on Pesach

Though who shall have the right
to write her faith that gives that right
past ego of choosing her

I mean: I think it gave even God guilt
when she labored to cremate
the suicides, the starved, the ill

I mean: she chose to survive by that work
for three years for love of God
whose laws command: endure

She who says she would not forget
though she live as long as God
one like any on the street who outlives him

She who now prays to Solomon's God
twenty-five centuries old in Jerusalem
and who now plants the olive

And yet I know that I too have worn the yarmulke
baffled as her children
to be the chosen of God

OUT OF EGYPT

1 Promised Land

So had not the Testament said
that my people in the desert ate no bread
and were given the Commandments

And at the 59th Street station of the express
the old Jew pretzel man blames each man
and smokes at the DO NOT SMOKE sign

And surely the poor are not free
yet had I not thought as one obsessed
that he too thinks that he shall profit—nonetheless

2 Exodus

Skull-capped boys talking ball scores
black beards in black overcoats and fedoras
among Italians, Ukrainians, and Chinese

Where the B train bolts Brooklyn
where a dark-eyed fidgety girl blurts though no car comes:
Mister, mister, cross me, mister

Amazed, I am she decades back, but daughter
what first-born stranger to Israel
still leads you before the gentile

3 Pharaoh

In Flatbush at the tarred-over trolley tracks
I went back to the doors of many dreams
though I could decipher no bell

Nor remember no night nor dream
where in a photo I sleep with my bear
where my parents sleep and breathe

But I had pitched pennies
traded baseball cards, played stickball, hoarded marbles
where Turner Place was vast dirt and weeds

Just as under Ocean Parkway in the sealed tunnel
my teddy, my bed, my broom-handle bat
wait to bear me through the underworld

THE AWAKENED

From the start a baby grabs his crib bars
though the snake the fly the crocodile
would cut him bind him beat him

And he fall between the blue sky and the black sky
onto the road of red fire
though he loves the sun

For the wind saved him from the belly
he does not want to dream under
the ocean where a corpse floats

He hates his voice like the bee's
like the cat's hiss in the dark
like the hoot of the owl shut from its house

He kicks out and loathes his body curled
as if his mouth were the anus
that sucks its own excrement

He longs for the breath of his chest
to be rubbed in oil as with his own sweat
he loves to hold his penis

He does not want sleep with no window and door
his lips stiff his fingers bent
death sits so close at a breast

For if he cries who should bless his crying
or hear his teeth grind
or soothe his hot throat

For from the start a baby fears
the snake of his name and the fly of his eye
and the crocodile who tears his shadow

These ones of his arm and his leg
whose small bricks would be his spine
he who has so few hairs on his head

HYMN

So thus shall the lion brush his tail to the fly at the flood Nile
    to feed
on day one of year one before the white Sirius risen at the dawn
clear as the chisel on the granite of the temple of the zodiac
    of Isis
where a Pharaoh had suckled at Hathor under the Great Bear

And Orion of the green-faced feathered judge Osiris of the
    dead
who lie and implore and swear for his mercy
curled in Egypt in their incense in the earth dug up by the dog
eight thousand years ago like the fetus in my dream of the
    blue closet

And I saw in the dark the hawk head at the head of my
    father the engineer
who had courted with the gilt-edged Victorian sonnets in
    leather
like the equations of a war that was never to be won between
    a man and a woman

As Horus alone had been allowed the sky to drowse long in
    blood's afterburn
with the cow from Dendera before the ibis and the jackal
at his altar arisen from the hawk perch
at the reed pool as he was swaddled like a Moses from the
    crocodile

Whoever she was drinking coffee over the dusk of the Hudson
eyelids tinted silver, sunburnt in underwear

adorned with gold and lapis and the cobra or armored like
    the Amazon

For I had been the circumcised as if drugged before the heat
    of the mouth of
the gentile combing her gold hair at the floors and floors of
    the city
because Israel had always wandered and warred as the idolators
of the cow head in the desert on the pillar

In the indecipherable light of the living photographed
on my shoulders by my father at the marbles on black dirt
    like the stars
that the priests of the Mother had watched through the
    notch of the palm leaf

Imprinted at the eye from their light years under the white
    insomniac continents
cracked in the wall when the sexual worm shall pearl the sheet
    with its inch
as I tried to open the light of my own hand
to the child who had not eaten though a family had been fed

When the trolley had plunged to the tunnel on Church Avenue
and I read as a boy scout of the Draco Patrol
the book in my bed in my parents' room
of the time traveler who had killed his ancestor when Thuban
    had been the pole

When even the excrement might have flared like the crown
    of the eclipse
and any Greek bored with the Greek might have tracked the
    lion
that Samson had made kneel to spare the parched ground

That is never too high or too low to be changed to the silt
      of the Delta
as the gold is turned from the iron under the blood Antares
and the violet is raised against the ruby lily and the cardinal

Even though I had seen the wasp in the web impale the spider
or had thought and thought before the female fish in the
      museum
that shrivels the male to nothing but dead genitals

As the priests at Philae of Isis below the cataract
had sacrificed the red-haired Set who had fed the crab the
      phallus of Osiris
smeared with her natron in the blackest radiation of the
      brains and viscera
for his worship as the phoenix at Heliopolis with Ra

As all are commanded to yield like the mummy when the
      dung beetle rolls the sun
before all the befores of the trillions of nights past night
      and day
though I knew that the broken receding mouth of the Sphinx
      had nothing to add
of resurrection in the history of its grimace

For any art, love, or politic
of the human that had refused us so that I cried from the
      human
Goddess Goddess Goddess of the sistrum of Abaton, Senem,
      and Elephantine

Ordained once to your first irreducible face of the nubile
twenty centuries past Christ at the fourteen year old with
      oiled pubic hair

in Brooklyn in a yellow sweater
luminous as the blue double of Pharaoh the *ka* in the dark
   when I touched her

HUGH SEIDMAN was born in Brooklyn, New York, and holds degrees in mathematics and theoretical physics as well as an MFA from Columbia University. His poetry has won several awards, including a CAPS Grant, an NEA Creative Writing Fellowship and the Yale Series of Younger Poets Prize for his first book, *Collecting Evidence*. *Blood Lord*, his second book, was published in 1974. He has taught and been a writer-in-residence at many colleges and universities including Yale, the New School for Social Research, the City College of CUNY, Washington College, the University of Wisconsin, and the College of William and Mary. He lives in New York City.